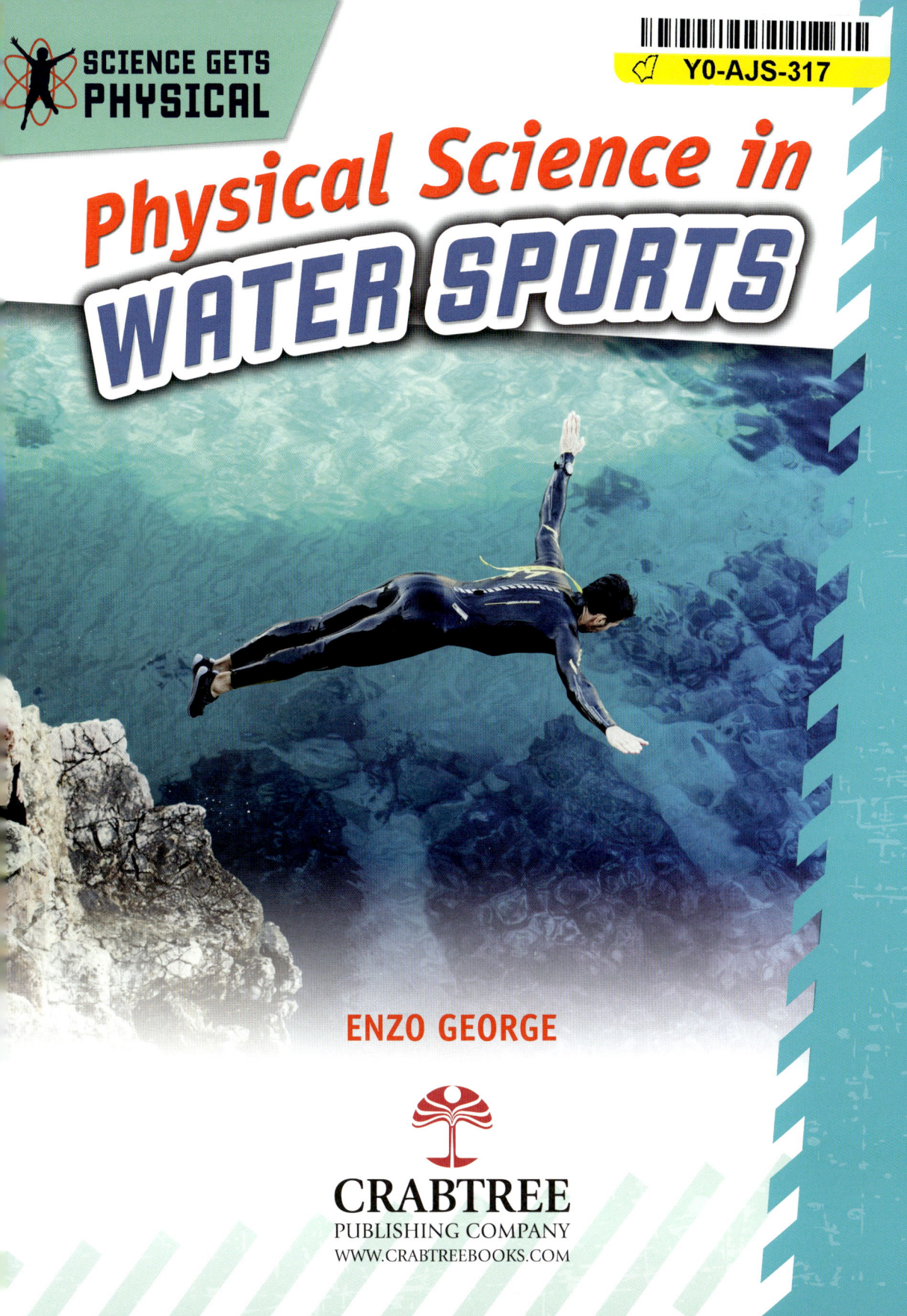

SCIENCE GETS PHYSICAL

Physical Science in WATER SPORTS

ENZO GEORGE

CRABTREE
PUBLISHING COMPANY
WWW.CRABTREEBOOKS.COM

Author: Enzo George
Editors: Sarah Eason, Jennifer Sanderson, and Elizabeth DiEmanuele
Consultant: David Hawksett
Editorial director: Kathy Middleton
Proofreader: Wendy Scavuzzo
Design: Paul Myerscough and Jeni Child
Design edits: Katherine Berti
Cover design: Lorraine Inglis
Photo research: Rachel Blount
Print and production coordinator: Katherine Berti

Written, developed, and produced by Calcium

Photo Credits:
t=Top, c=Center, b=Bottom, l= Left, r=Right
Inside: Shutterstock: Pierre-Yves Babelon: p. 35b; Darren Baker: p. 36; Paolo Bona: p. 5, 17t, 19, 22; BrunoRosa: p. 16–17b; Andrey Burmakin: p. 15; Ronnie Chua: p. 4; Corepics VOF: p. 30b; Artur Didyk: p. 25; Martina Ebel: p. 26; Joel Everard: p. 42–43t; Evocation Images: p. 38; Gaborturcsi: p. 34–35t; Andy Gin: p. 45; Mitch Gunn: p. 21; Steve Heap: p. 39; Icealex: p. 1, 18; J_K: p. 7; Purmak Marina: p. 42b; Microgen: p. 9, 10, 23, 28; Ohrim: p. 40; Pavel L Photo and Video: p. 8; Sergey Peterman: p. 12; AL Robinson: p. 29; Shch: p. 37; Sirtravelalot: p. 14, 20, 27; Ivan Smuk: p. 24; Akepong Srichaichana: p. 44; Sunnypicsoz: p. 33t; Trubavin: p. 41; VideoTD: p. 30–31t; XiXinXing: p. 6; YanLev: p. 3, 32–33b; Leonard Zhukovsky: p. 13; Wikimedia Commons: Craig Maccubbin: p. 11
Cover: Shutterstock: Microgen

Library and Archives Canada Cataloguing in Publication

Title: Physical science in water sports / Enzo George.
Names: George, Enzo, author.
Description: Series statement: Science gets physical | Includes index.
Identifiers: Canadiana (print) 20190195495 | Canadiana (ebook) 20190195517 | ISBN 9780778775560 (hardcover) | ISBN 9780778776529 (softcover) | ISBN 9781427125248 (HTML)
Subjects: LCSH: Aquatic sports—Juvenile literature.
Classification: LCC GV770.5 .G46 2020 | DDC j797—dc23

Library of Congress Cataloging-in-Publication Data

Names: George, Enzo, author.
Title: Physical science in water sports / Enzo George.
Description: New York, New York : Crabtree Publishing Company, [2020] | Series: Science gets physical | Includes index.
Identifiers: LCCN 2019043595 (print) | LCCN 2019043596 (ebook) | ISBN 9780778775560 (hardcover) | ISBN 9780778776529 (paperback) | ISBN 9781427125248 (ebook)
Subjects: LCSH: Water sports--Juvenile literature. | Physical sciences--Juvenile literature.
Classification: LCC GV770.5 .G46 2020 (print) | LCC GV770.5 (ebook) | DDC 787.2--dc23
LC record available at https://lccn.loc.gov/2019043595
LC ebook record available at https://lccn.loc.gov/2019043596

Crabtree Publishing Company
www.crabtreebooks.com   1-800-387-7650

Printed in the U.S.A./012020/CG20191115

Copyright © **2020 CRATREE PUBLISHING COMPANY**. All rights reserved. No part of this publication may be reproduced, stored in a retrieval system or be transmitted in any form or by any means, electronic, mechanical, photocopying, recording, or otherwise, without the prior written permission of Crabtree Publishing Company. In Canada: We acknowledge the financial support of the Government of Canada through the Canada Book Fund for our publishing activities.

Published in Canada
Crabtree Publishing
616 Welland Ave.
St. Catharines, Ontario
L2M 5V6

Published in the United States
Crabtree Publishing
PMB 59051
350 Fifth Avenue, 59th Floor
New York, New York 10118

Published in the United Kingdom
Crabtree Publishing
Maritime House
Basin Road North, Hove
BN41 1WR

Published in Australia
Crabtree Publishing
Unit 3 - 5 Currumbin Court
Capalaba
QLD 4157

CONTENTS

CHAPTER 1 WORLD OF WATER 4
Staying Afloat 6

CHAPTER 2 SWIMMING 8
Thrust and Drag 10
Choose Your Stroke 12
The Front Crawl 14
Water Polo 16

CHAPTER 3 DIVING 18
Gravity and Acceleration 20
Torque 22

CHAPTER 4 PADDLING SPORTS 24
Boats and Blades 26
Oarlocks and Levers 28
Top Speed 30

CHAPTER 5 SAILING 32
Shape of the Hull 34
Sails and Keels 36
Tacking 38

CHAPTER 6 SURFING 40
Board and Balance 42

GET PHYSICAL! 44
GLOSSARY 46
LEARNING MORE 47
INDEX 48

CHAPTER 1
WORLD OF WATER

The water is a great place for sports and activities. You can hang out with your friends or family at the beach, canoe across a lake, or even swim in a pool.

Have you ever wondered why a high-dive that would kill you on land is possible in water? Or why the front crawl is the fastest swimming stroke? Or how paddles work as **levers** and push a canoe forward? That's where **physics** comes in. Physics is the science that helps us answer these questions and more.

A Range of Sports

Around the world, people enjoy the ocean for swimming or for surfing on huge waves that come crashing down into shallow water and sand. They might try a type of sailboat, such as a **dinghy** that holds one or two people, or a high-tech ocean racer. Ocean racers carry crews of 10 or more people at great speeds in races that can be as far as around the world.

The beautiful waters of Lake Louise in the Rocky Mountains in Canada are perfect for exploring by canoe.

Swimming can be a lot of fun, but more serious swimmers can attend regular swim meets or competitions.

Some people use rivers or lakes for swimming or for paddling sports, such as kayaking, canoeing, and rowing (sometimes known as crew). There are straight rowing courses that are straight for 1.2 miles (2 km) long, and wide enough for at least eight boats to race side by side. Kayakers tackle **whitewater** rapids in rivers or practice their skills in human-made waterways that create a range of challenges.

In the Pool

In warm places, many homes have their own swimming pools. Families swim, do water exercises, or just hang out. In colder places, outdoor pools are not as popular. However, there are also large public swimming pools people use for laps, which is swimming up and down the length of the pool. Some pools have diving boards that are up to 33 feet (10 m) in the air. That is very high! There are also pools that are more for fun, with water slides and wave machines, where lifeguards do not blow their whistles to make swimmers stay in their lanes.

Staying Afloat

Humans have always been attracted to the water. Maybe this is unsurprising, because life on Earth began in the water billions of years ago. More than 70 percent of Earth's surface is covered in water. Water is also important for supporting life and makes up at least 60 percent of our bodies. Water is literally in our blood.

Flotation aids help you float. They are filled with air because it is less dense than water or the human body.

Nature of Water

Water is made from **molecules** that are formed by **atoms** of hydrogen and oxygen. The molecules are close together, making water thicker than air and the human body, because our lungs are filled with air. This means that water has a **force** of **buoyancy** that helps the body float. The buoyancy force pushes the human body up against the pull of **gravity**, the force that pulls objects toward Earth's center.

Floating makes our bodies feel as though they are lighter in water than they are on land. Water also helps a lot of other things float, from pool noodles to surfboards, kayaks and canoes, rowing boats, and sailboats. Sailboats speed across the surface of the water, cutting through waves.

GETTING PHYSICAL: A EUREKA MOMENT

In the third century B.C.E., the Greek mathematician Archimedes made a discovery. He figured out that objects placed in water displace their own weight. This means that water moves out of the way for an object. The amount of water that is displaced is the same as the buoyancy force acting on the object. The object sinks into the water until it reaches the **equilibrium point**. The equilibrium point is where the weight pulling the object down is the same as the buoyancy force pushing it up.

Buoyancy and Drag

Physics affects water sports differently than land sports. This is because of the differences between water and air. The **density** (thickness) of molecules that help us float is also what makes it harder for an object to move forward in water. This resistance in water is also known as **drag.** Most water sports take advantage of the buoyancy force, while decreasing the drag forces of the water.

Sea water is full of particles of salts and other chemicals. The salts and chemicals make it denser than fresh water. They also increase the buoyancy force in the ocean. These salts and other chemicals make it easier to float, but the water is "thicker" and harder to swim through.

Surfboards allow surfers to ride over waves without sinking.

CHAPTER 2

SWIMMING

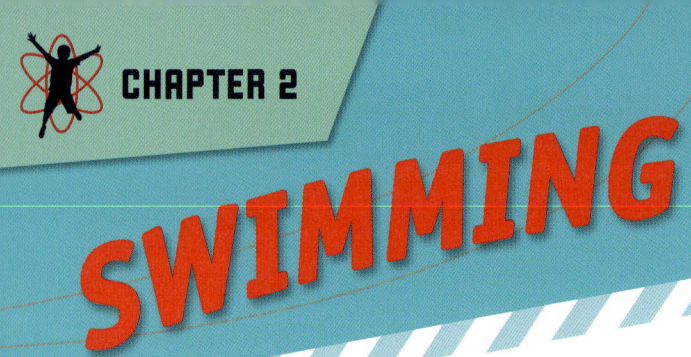

Getting in the water can be fun! A cool swim on a hot day is always refreshing. You can also play in the pool with your friends. You might be more energetic and swim some laps in a larger pool, for exercise or to make the swim team. When you learn to swim, what you are really doing is learning the physics of being in the water.

Floating Around

Humans float in water. That is because our bodies, with lungs filled with air, are less dense than water. That means that the buoyancy force lifts our bodies to the surface.

Swimmers dive into a pool at the start of a race. Swim competitions have four strokes: front crawl, butterfly, breaststroke, and backstroke.

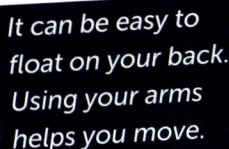

It can be easy to float on your back. Using your arms helps you move.

If you have ever tried to float, you may know it is easier if you move your arms and legs. They "push" against the water and help raise your equilibrium point, where the forces of buoyancy and gravity balance. This balance keeps you from sinking to the bottom.

The buoyancy force acts through the **center of mass** of the **submerged** part of your body. This means that it goes through the middle part of your body's weight under the water. If it goes through a different part, your body will rotate in the water until it lines up with your center of mass. You can stop this from happening by spreading out. You can also move your arms and legs to push against the water.

From Floating to Swimming

Floating is different from swimming. To swim, you need to position your body so that you can push water behind you. According to scientist Isaac Newton's Third Law of Motion, this creates an equal reaction force in the opposite direction, so you can move forward.

Thrust and Drag

Racing swimmers compete in four strokes: front crawl, backstroke, breaststroke, and butterfly. But there are many other strokes that will move a swimmer through the water, such as the dog paddle or sidestroke. What all swimming strokes have in common is that they allow swimmers to generate a force, called thrust, that pushes them through the water.

Moving Force

Swimmers use their arms and legs to create thrust. A swimmer's speed depends on the strength of the thrust they generate. To move forward, the swimmer has to overcome the drag force generated by the water. As the swimmer's body moves forward, a thin layer of molecules in the water clings to the part of their body that is submerged. The water molecules create drag that holds the swimmer back. Because water is denser than air, a swimmer experiences more drag in the water than someone who is walking or running through the air.

A swimmer's cap is tight to make a smooth surface. This surface creates less drag than their hair, helping the swimmer to move through the water faster.

Overcoming Drag

Another cause of drag is the swimmer's arm movements through the water. The movements increase the amount of drag, because the water molecules cling to their arms. In that way, the water "pushes back" as the swimmer pushes water out of the way. A third cause is wave drag, which is the name given to the drag generated by the waves caused by a swimmer moving through the water. The quickest swimmers are those who can create the most thrust force, while at the same time reducing the drag they experience. Good swimmers are able to do this by generating **lift** when they swim. This force raises their body in the water, reducing the amount of skin that is submerged. This reduces drag, because fewer water molecules cling to the swimmers' bodies.

GETTING PHYSICAL: MODERN RACING SUITS

One way that scientists help swimmers go faster is by designing new swimsuits. At the Beijing Olympics in 2008, most medals were won by swimmers who wore rubberized, full-body suits like those shown on the right. The suits compressed their bodies into tubelike shapes that reduced the drag effect of water on the swimmers' bodies. It gave swimmers such an advantage, that by the start of 2010, the suits were banned. Today's suits must be made of certain materials and cannot cover a swimmer's body below the knee. Swimwear manufacturers have continued to come up with new designs. They test designs by scanning swimmers' bodies and using computers to model the flow of water. Scientists also designed goggles to make them more **streamlined**, and swim caps to cling to a swimmer's head as closely and smoothly as possible.

Choose Your Stroke

One of the most spectacular sights in the pool is the 50 m freestyle sprint. The swimmers dive in, low and flat, and disappear underwater for a few seconds. Beneath the surface, they use two-legged dolphin kicks. These are when swimmers kick from the knees to generate power. Once the swimmers come back to the surface, everyone races to the far end of the pool.

Fast Strokes

The race is called "freestyle" because it is open to swimmers using any stroke. Most swimmers use the front crawl because that is the fastest of all the strokes. The next fastest is the butterfly. The butterfly stroke is when swimmers combine dolphin kicks with arms that pull back and rotate out of the water together. The stroke is tiring, because it takes a lot of **energy** to pull the swimmer's body out of the water.

Butterfly uses the most energy of all the swimming strokes, because the swimmer constantly uses muscles in their arms and legs at the same time.

Two More Strokes

In the backstroke, the swimmer lies on their back and rotates their arms. While one arm is in the air, the other is pulling through the water, like a windmill. The swimmer reaches as far as possible in front of their head to "grab" the water, then they pull the water back behind their body.

In the breaststroke, the swimmer uses both arms together. They push their arms in front, then pull them back. Then they bring their hands together in front of their chest. At the same time, the swimmer's legs do a froglike kick. Breaststroke is the easiest stroke for swimmers who want to swim long distances.

SCIENCE WINS!

MICHAEL PHELPS

Michael Phelps is probably the greatest swimmer of all time. He won a record 23 Olympic gold medals in his career. He won eight gold medals at the 2008 Beijing Olympic Games, a record for any single Olympics. He also won gold in the individual medley, a race in which swimmers do all four strokes. In this photo, he is swimming breaststroke in the medley. Part of Phelps's success is because of his body shape. He has a thin torso and relatively short legs that reduce drag through the water. He also has a huge arm span of 6 feet 7 inches (2 m). His size-14 feet are big enough to act like flippers and helped him generate power.

The Front Crawl

A swimmer using the front crawl reaches forward with their hand to "grab" the water and pull it back past their body.

The fastest swimming stroke is the front crawl. Swimmers barely raise their heads to breathe, as their arms take turns cutting through the water. They remain as smooth as possible. One of the reasons front crawlers go so fast is the same force that keeps airplanes in the air: lift.

Generating Power

The front crawl relies on arm strength. Although the legs add kick, they mostly make sure the swimmer moves in a straight line down the pool. An important part about the front crawl is the swimmer's hands. These change position during the stroke so that they are always pushing the water backward, not up or down. This strengthens the forward thrust.

Getting a Lift

The position of the hands acts like airplane wings. The forces acting on the hand are broken down into lift and drag forces. Lift force happens from the water having to travel farther over the hand than underneath it. Drag happens from the hand and lower part of the arm moving through the water. These lift and drag forces are the squared **velocity** of the swimmer and the water. Velocity is the speed an object goes in one direction.

A Question of Angles

Swimmers angle their hands to lower drag as they move through the water. They do what they can to stay in position. Since each arm alternates strokes, a swimmer's body sometimes moves a little bit. To stay in position, swimmers will keep their arms as tight as possible to their bodies, which reduces drag and lessens the area that pushes against the water.

GETTING PHYSICAL: CATCH YOUR BREATH

If you watch a race, you will notice that swimmers don't take their heads out of the water, even to breathe. Keeping their heads in the water pushes a "hole" and keeps them as smooth as possible. As shown in this photo, swimmers turn their head as they swim to raise only their face out of the water. They often only breathe with their mouths. The speed they create means that water flows past their mouth, not into it. The speed lets them breathe without getting a mouthful of pool water.

Water Polo

Water polo is one of the hardest water sports. For one thing, it is very rough. Players crash into one another underwater as they try to grab the ball. For another, the pool is too deep for players to stand on the bottom. They have to tread water.

Treading Water

Treading water takes a lot of effort. It is far harder to float in the pool if you are upright. When you are lying on your back, the area of your body touching the water is bigger. There is a stronger buoyancy force that helps you float. When you are upright, the gravity pulling you is the same, but the buoyant force is much smaller. You have to move your arms near the surface of the water and kick your feet to create lift.

Water polo players need strong arm muscles to be able to throw the ball over long distances.

Throwing the Ball

In water polo, two teams of seven players compete. The goals are at each end of the pool. The ball has a **mass** of 1 pound (0.45 kg). The top players can throw it at a velocity of 72 feet per second (23 m/s). It is more likely that a player would throw it at about 49 feet per second (15 m/s). At this velocity, it would take less than two seconds to travel the length of a 98-foot (30 m) pool. When throwing the ball, players need to reach as high out of the water as possible. They also need to throw the ball hard because it is heavy and wet. The water adds mass. The ball also needs to overcome **air resistance** and push away the molecules of the air. Players need to be out of the water when they throw. If not, the water creates a heavy drag force on their throwing arm and slows it down. The slower their arm travels, the more force they have to generate to achieve the same speed for the ball.

GETTING PHYSICAL: SYNCHRONIZED SWIMMING

In synchronized swimming, swimmers also have to tread water. Two or more swimmers do a set of moves at the same time, like a dance team. Outside of the water, routines look graceful and easy. In reality, effort is happening under the water. Swimmers have to work hard with their legs or arms to hold themselves in position.

CHAPTER 3

DIVING

Diving depends on gravity. Gravity acts on the mass of a diver and pulls them down toward the water. For the best high divers, the drop allows them to do somersaults and twists before they enter the water. They try to do this without creating a splash. A splash happens when the diver's legs rotate forward or backward from the **perpendicular**. In competitions, divers win points for a clean entry into the water.

Avoiding Injury

Entering the water cleanly is not only important because it looks good. Water is about 400 times denser than air, because the molecules that make it up are pressed closer together. That means water is far more resistant to allowing the body to pass through it. When the body hits the water at high speed, it is almost like hitting a solid surface. The **impact** can break bones.

Cliff divers perform dives from great heights into deep water.

Hands Lead the Way

Divers use their hands and arms to enter the water first. Using their hands first creates a "hole" that lessens the impact felt by their head. Diving that way tightens the surface of the body and makes it as small as possible. There is less splash and resistance. A belly flop is different. It takes up the largest possible area when the body hits the water. There is a lot more resistance, which creates a huge splash! The resistance is why a belly flop hurts your stomach.

Types of Diving

There are two main types of diving. The first type is platform diving, which involves diving from a solid board or a rock above the water. The second type is springboard diving. A springboard is a long, flexible board. The diver bounces on one end. The board lifts the diver higher in the air as they jump and land. A springboard dive has upward velocity. The diver gets thrown into the air before gravity pulls them down.

A diver stands on their tiptoes ready to bounce at the end of a springboard.

Gravity and Acceleration

Any dive where the diver performs somersaults and twists is a race against time and gravity. The diver has to be efficient. They need to finish their tricks and have an entry position by the time they meet the water. A dive from the 33-foot (10 m) board takes about 1.42 seconds.

In the Air

Once a diver is in the air, there is nothing they can do to make the dive last longer. The only force acting on the diver's body is gravity. Small changes in body mass or in air resistance do not make much difference in a short dive.

The velocity of a diver increases as they fall. The diver hits the water with more force when diving from a greater height. Newton's Second Law of Motion explains why this happens. It says that force = mass x **acceleration**. The equation means that the more mass and acceleration there is, the greater the force. The increased force is why the diver needs to enter hands first.

Seeing the Surface

There are special pools for diving competitions. These pools have machines in the walls that make bubbles on the water. For divers, it can be hard to see the water from the top of the high board. The bubbles let divers know where the surface of the water is.

When a diver jumps and lands on a springboard, the board throws them into the air with more force. The diver gains height to perform maneuvers.

In synchronized diving, athletes perform the same dive with the same timing.

GETTING PHYSICAL: MINIMIZING IMPACT

The highest dives into a pool are from 33-foot (10 m) boards, but cliff divers can dive from heights of up to 85 feet (26 m). These dives can last up to three seconds, meaning cliff divers hit the water with more force than pool divers. Gravity accelerates the divers toward the water. Their speed increases by 32 feet per second (9.8 m/s), every second. The longer the diver's fall, the faster they fall until they reach their highest speed, called **terminal velocity**. When divers hit the water, their speed drops to near zero. This sudden **deceleration** produces g force. G force is a measure of the pull on the body based on the normal gravity on Earth (1 g). Cliff divers experience 2 or 3 gs as they decelerate on hitting the water.

Torque

The secret to a successful dive is to do as many tricks as possible before positioning to enter the water. It looks graceful, but it is also a demonstration of physical forces.

Types of Momentum

A diver in the air has two types of **momentum**. Momentum is the quantity of motion, measured as mass x velocity. One type of momentum is linear momentum, the force that keeps the diver's body traveling straight downward. The other is angular momentum, the energy that causes the body to rotate and continue rotating. An example of angular momentum is a somersault. Angular momentum relates to the diver's angular velocity (how fast they spin). To make angular momentum, the diver needs to generate **torque**. Torque is a force that makes things rotate, as the diver leaves the board. The diver cannot generate torque in the air as there is nothing to push against.

Divers fold their arms and legs together in the pike position to increase their speed in the air.

Using Inertia

The moment of inertia is another part of diving. This is the object's rotational mass (the part that makes an object hard to rotate). This means the higher an object's moment of inertia, the harder it is to make it turn. The moment of inertia depends on both its mass and position in relation to the **rotation point**. The farther a mass is from the point of rotation, the higher its moment of inertia. To understand this, think of a ballet dancer spinning on one leg: they spin faster once they pull their arms closer to their body.

Hitting the Water

In the air, the diver can use the moment of inertia to change their angular velocity (how fast they spin). When the diver somersaults, the point of rotation is near the center of their body. If the diver tucks their arms and legs in, more of their mass is at the rotation point. This lowers the moment of inertia and increases their speed. A tighter tuck creates a faster rotation. When it is time to hit the water, the diver stretches their body out again. This movement increases the moment of inertia and lowers the angular velocity.

A diver slows down in the water as the air they push beneath the surface creates a stream of bubbles.

SCIENCE WINS!

THE 513XD

In 2017, engineers at Sydney University in Australia used math to figure out a new dive, called the 513XD. They built a computer model of how the human body twists and somersaults in the air. Then, they came up with a new way of generating movements in the air. The dive they designed had 1.5 somersaults and 5 twists. The problem is that it would take 1.8 seconds. The longest a diver has in the air with a big jump upward off the board is 1.6 seconds. They believe there may be ways to speed up the turns, such as by using tight pike positions when the diver bends at the waist to bring their arms and legs together in front of them. So far, no diver has performed the 513XD in public.

CHAPTER 4

PADDLING SPORTS

One of the earliest ways humans traveled on seas and rivers was by canoe. Canoes were long, simple boats, shaped from logs and pushed by flat blades connected to long paddles.

What Is the Difference?

There are a number of different ways to get around using paddles. The physics are similar in each case. In canoeing, paddlers kneel or sit on a seat or crossbar in the bottom of the boat. They propel themselves with a single paddle, which they use on both sides of the boat to travel in a straight line.

Kayaking is similar, but the paddler sits on the bottom of the boat with their legs out in front. Kayakers use a long paddle with blades on each end. They use a windmilling rotation of their arms to pull alternately on each side of the boat.

In a rowing eight, the boat is pushed by four oars on each side, which keep it moving in a straight line.

In a kayak, paddlers use an elasticated skirt around their waist that seals the top of the boat to stop it from filling with water.

Rowing Boats

In rowing, from two to eight rowers pull on a single oar each. The oars pass through an arm on the side of the boat to pull the blade through the water. The arm acts as a **fulcrum**, so the oar works as a lever, multiplying the force generated by the rower. Rowers often have seats that slide on runners. These allow them to bend and straighten their legs to generate more power. They sit with their backs toward the direction they travel, so boats often have a cox to steer. The cox is a crew member who sits at the rear of the boat and looks forward. Sculling is a version of rowing in which each rower has two oars, one on each side of the boat.

Rowing is a very fast sport. The boats are made to move as fast as possible, using the force of up to eight rowers. The boats are fragile, so they are useful for racing only on flat water and straight courses.

Canoes and kayaks are also used for racing, but they can go on more than just flat water. They can travel on whitewater, which is fast and shallow. They are also used in specialized travel, such as slalom, in which paddlers follow a course of gates through rough water.

Boats and Blades

The science behind paddling sports is based on the three laws of motion. In the 1600s, English scientist Isaac Newton came up with them. These laws explain the way everything in the universe moves.

The Second Law

As shared in chapter three, Newton's Second Law states that force = mass x acceleration. For paddling, this means the boat should be as light as possible. A lighter boat reduces the force needed to move it through the water. Canoes and kayaks are made from light materials and are long and thin. They move through the water with little resistance. Their helps spread the weight of the paddlers over a greater area. This means the paddlers' mass is not all in one spot.

The Third Law

Newton's Third Law says that for every action, there is an equal and opposite reaction. This is true of all motion. For example, when a runner pushes their foot against the ground, the ground pushes back with an equal force. The exchange causes them to move up and forward. The ground itself does not change. With a paddle or oar, as the blade pushes backward against the water, the water pushes back with a forward force that powers the boat's motion.

On smooth water, paddlers alternate paddling with the blade on each side of the oar.

Using the Blade

The blade is a large, flat area at the end of a **cylindrical** paddle. The paddler gains the most force when they do a power stroke. This stroke happens when the paddle is perpendicular to the flow of the water. The paddler pulls hard and pushes the water back. This creates forward momentum. To get the blade in and out of the water, it is easiest to move it sideways up and down. There is less water resistance on its edges. This is why paddlers turn their paddles. They keep the blade perpendicular during the stroke. Then, flat the remaining time.

Blades for whitewater have a curve to give them a larger surface area and more "grip" on the water.

GETTING PHYSICAL: STREAMLINING

Canoes, kayaks, and rowing boats have the same basic shape. They come together in a point at the front and back, while widening smoothly around the middle. This basic shape makes traveling through water as smooth as possible. The front, or **bow**, of the boat pushes through the water. As it does this, the water flows along the sides and past the back. When it moves quickly, the water creates a wave alongside the boat, which can slow it down. One of the reasons canoes and other personal boats are so long is to lessen the **turbulence** created by waves. The shape reduces drag, which helps the boat cut through the water.

Oarlocks and Levers

In kayaks, paddlers learn to keep their arms out in front of them to power the stroke with their full upper body. This includes the small of their backs, their chests, shoulders, and arms!

Moving Parts

In rowing, or crew, there is a different technique to increase the power of the stroke. The technique uses the whole human body, including the biggest muscles: the thighs. In a rowing shell, each rower has their own seat, which rolls on small wheels across short slides. The long oar is around 12 feet (3.7 m) long. It is held in place by a bracket called an oarlock. The oarlock is attached to the end of an arm that extends from the side of the boat. These arms are normally on both sides of the boat, from the front to the back.

The oar is a lever that pivots around the oarlock. As the rower pulls the oars backward, the blades sweep forward through the water.

The oarlocks act as fulcrums. They turn the momentum of the rowers into momentum in the opposite direction. When rowers slide forward on their seats, their oars sweep back through the air behind them. At the greatest forward point of the slide, the rower lowers the blade vertically into the water. This is called "the catch." The rower straightens their legs and, as this happens, the oarlock transfers the backward motion into a forward sweep through the water. To finish the stroke, the rower uses the momentum of the blade to pull the oar with their arms through to their chest. Then they lower their hands and raise the blade back out of the water, and slide forward to start the next stroke.

Multiplying Force

There are only two points of the stroke that do not move: the oarlock and the rower's feet. The rower's feet are in shoes attached to the hull of the boat. The oarlock and feet act as fulcrums. The oarlock and the rower's body act as levers that create as much force as possible. This allows the boat's center of gravity to move forward and backward. (The rowers' weight makes up about 80 percent of the boat's mass.) As a result, the boat rises and sinks at the front, which makes the boat travel faster and then slower during the stroke.

GETTING PHYSICAL: SLIDING SEATS

A rowing seat sits on four pairs of small wheels that anchor it to runners. This allows the seat to slide forward and backward as the rower does the stroke. The wheels are made of hard rubber or plastic. They contain ball **bearings** that let them rotate on their axles with almost no **friction**.

The result is that the rowers move back and forth with almost no resistance. This allows them to transmit the most power but also means that the boat's center of mass moves forward and backward. This causes the boat to alternately rise and sink at the front, leading to the boat traveling alternately quicker then slower during the stroke.

Top Speed

In the world of rowing, the eight is the fastest boat in the world. The eight includes eight rowers and a cox.

Record Breaking

To generate power, rowers tend to be tall, so they can take advantage of leverage during the stroke. They also tend to be heavy, because as Newton's Second Law says, force = mass x acceleration. A rower with larger mass can generate more force than one with a smaller mass at the same acceleration. Lighter rowers can get more power by rowing faster, or increasing their rating, or strokes per minute. All members of a crew have to move back and forth together, so everyone has to row at the rating of the slowest rower.

At the start of a race, rowers take a series of short strokes by keeping their back straight and not pulling the oar right through to their stomach.

GETTING PHYSICAL: WEIGHT DISTRIBUTION

In eights, crews often arrange the rowers. They put the lightest individuals in seats one, two, and three. The heaviest rowers tend to occupy seats four, five, and six, while the fittest and best technical rowers take the seven and stroke seats. When the boat is at its top speed, this allows its front to lift slightly out of the water. This lift is called hydroplaning. Hydroplaning reduces the amount of the hull's surface that is in contact with the water. This reduces drag and increases speed.

Setting the Pace

At the start of a race, the crew raises its velocity from zero by taking a series of short, very rapid strokes. These strokes happen at a rating of up to 45 or even 50 for an eight. Once the boat moves, the crew settles into a steady rating of 38 to 40. Later in the race, a crew might raise the rating above 45 again for short bursts to try to pull ahead of an opponent.

The whole crew follows the speed set by the stroke, who rows nearest the **stern** of the boat. Even though the crew can see only the rower in front of them, all the rowers can see the stroke's oar and follow its pace. The cox also calls out ratings over a speaker system.

CHAPTER 5

SAILING

Sailing seems very simple: the wind blows into a canvas sail and pushes a boat across the water. Sailing has been developed over thousands of years to use the power of the wind, but that power would not be much use without understanding physics.

Sailors use harnesses to lean out of the opposite side of the boat to balance the force of the wind.

*A sailor tucks their body weight inside the hull. The helmsman uses a handle called a tiller to move the **rudder** in the water to steer.*

Catch the Wind

There is one thing that science will never be able to achieve. No one can make the wind blow if it is not blowing, or make it stop when it is. Winds are created by differences in **air pressure** in the atmosphere above Earth. Air moves from areas of high pressure to areas of lower pressure. Science cannot control the wind, but it has solved problems related to traveling on water. Sails are set up in a way that allows them to move in the direction of the wind.

The Hull

The hulls of boats lower the amount of drag they create in the water and from the air. The hulls are also stable enough to remain safe in huge waves. The material is very important. The hulls must be made of a material that is strong and flexible, such as wooden planks. Some larger racing boats are made from synthetic (artificial) materials. The lighter the boat, the less of its hull travels through the water rather than through the air.

On long-distance races, boats carry the latest navigation aids, such as a global positioning system (GPS) device. They have radios and video links, so they can stream images all over the world. But, some of the technology is the same as thousands of years ago. Even the most advanced boats can suffer from a broken mast.

Shape of the Hull

One of the best ways to speed up a sailboat is to reduce the forces that slow it down. Resistance from the water is one of them. As the hull of the vessel passes through the water, molecules of the water cling to the surface. These molecules form a stationary layer that moves with the boat through the water. As the couplings between the molecules of water break, this creates a force that slows down the boat.

The hull lifts out of the water as much as possible. This reduces the drag on its surface.

Staying Smooth

As the speed and surface of the boat increase, so does the force. This force is a type of friction. It is not possible to reduce the friction on water in the same way as on land. The only way to reduce it is to make sure the hull is as smooth as possible.

Hull smoothness can also help to reduce drag caused by turbulence. When a boat sails, the water flows past it in streams. As the boat speeds up, turbulence causes waves and **eddies**. This increases resistance and reduces the boat's energy.

Hull Shape

Another form of resistance comes from the amount of water the boat pushes out of the way as it moves forward. Making a boat as narrow as possible can help, but if it is too narrow, it will become unstable. There have been many versions of hull shape over the centuries. One modern design widens slowly from the pointed bow and remains wide near the stern. Sometimes it tapers to make sure that the stern does not create eddies that will slow the boat down.

GETTING PHYSICAL: THE CATAMARAN

Over the centuries, boatbuilders have come up with many ways to improve performance. One of the most popular versions is the catamaran. This boat has two parallel hulls joined by a flat deck. Each of the hulls is narrower than a normal yacht hull, because it does not have to fit accommodation for the crew (which is on the deck). This means that the hulls experience less resistance from the water, which improves acceleration. To double its speed from a slow start, a normal yacht, called a monohull, needs twice as much power as a catamaran. A catamaran is wider than a conventional yacht, making it more stable. But, the vessels displace more water than monohulls. This removes some of the advantages of reduced resistance.

Sails and Keels

One of the most important parts of a sailboat is one of the most obvious: the sail. Yet there is another part that is almost as important that is usually never seen. This is called the keel. The keel is a thin board or ridge that extends from the underside of the boat. The keel is parallel with the direction of travel. Without the keel, a boat would be almost impossible to sail.

Under Sail

The total speed a sailboat can achieve is set by its mass and the force it can generate from the wind. The wind will push it more if there is a larger area of sail or sails. Think of pirate ships in movies. **Galleons** needed many large sails because the ships were very heavy and required a large force to keep them moving through the water. At the same time, having too large an area of sail can also make a boat unstable. This is particularly true of narrow yachts and dinghies, which can turn over in high winds.

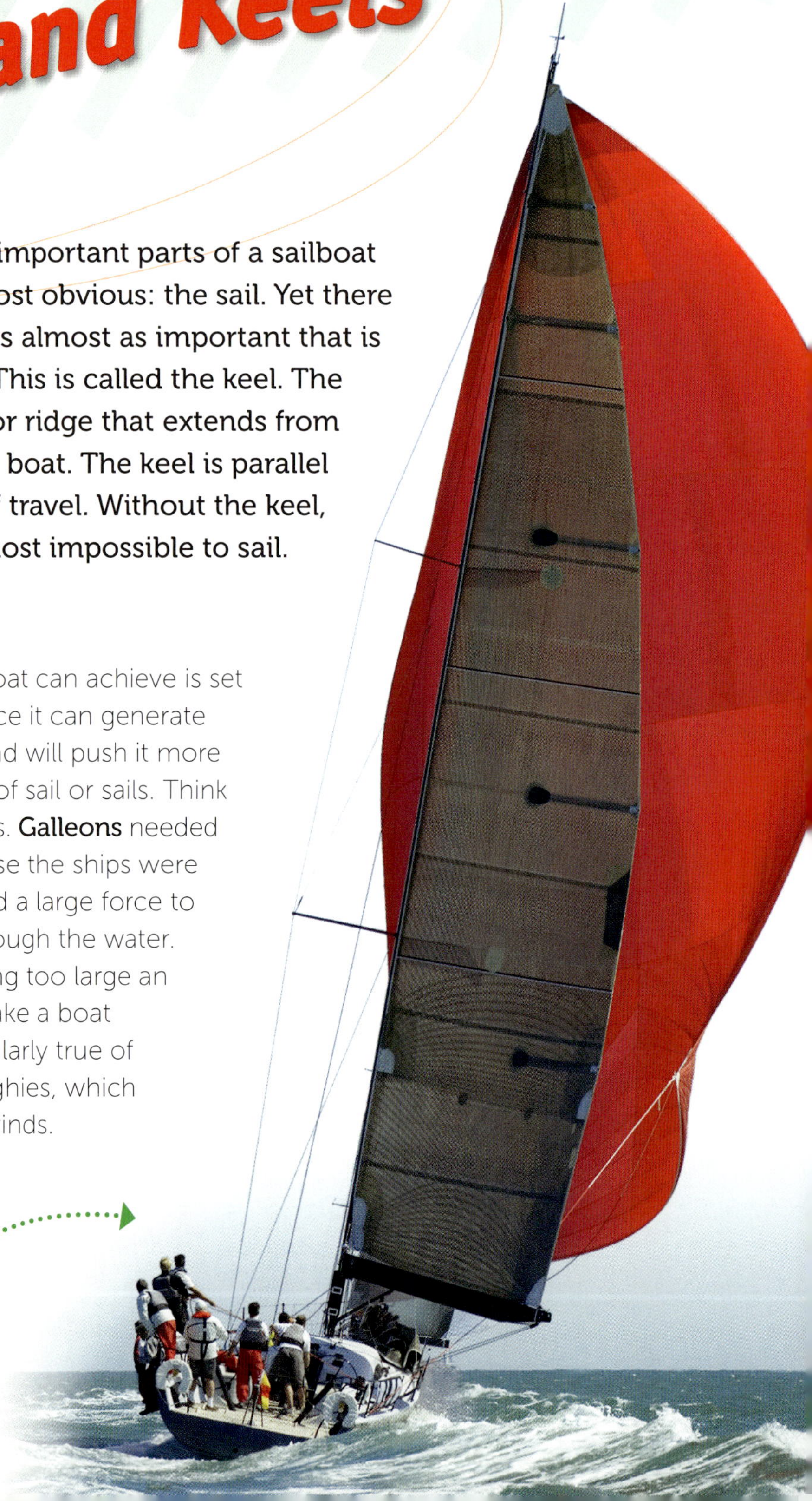

This yacht has a solid main sail on a boom to give it stability.

GETTING PHYSICAL: ROUND LEVERS

Large sails are heavy and wet sails are even heavier. It can take a lot of effort to pull large sheets of canvas up a mast. To do this, sailors use a complex series of ropes, known as rigging. With rigging, some ropes pass around many devices, such as pulleys or capstans, which are upright cylinders wound by a handle. In such a setup, a pulley or capstan acts as a fulcrum that magnifies the force carried by the rope. In the area of physics, the rope and the pulley act as the same basic type of machine as a seesaw: a lever.

To react to changing winds, sails can be rapidly taken down or put up. The upright mast holds up the main sails. They are also held in place at the bottom by a horizontal beam called a boom. The boom can swing around a full circle to catch the wind. Between the mast and the bow of the boat is often a second sail called a jib or headsail.

The Keel

The keel is vital because sailboats do not travel in a straight line through the water. They are always being pushed slightly sideways by the wind. As the wind pushes the boat in one direction, the keel pushes against the water. According to Newton's Third Law, this push back occurs with equal force. As a result, the boat travels on a steady course, not in the direction of the wind. The secret to a keel's effectiveness is its total area. Some keels are short but deep. Others are long and shallow.

The keel of a yacht is visible only when it is taken out of the water.

Tacking

It's easy to see how a sailboat travels with the wind behind it. An amazing thing about a sailboat is its ability to sail into the wind, even when it blows against it. To explain how this happens, physicists compare the sails to the airplane wing.

Creating Lift

Airplane wings work by creating lift. While the underneath of the wing is flat, the top of the wing is curved. This means that air that passes over the wing has to travel farther than air passing beneath the wing. For this reason, the air passing over the wing travels faster and creates a region of low pressure above the wing that "lifts" the wing into it. Lift happens with such force that it can overcome the force of gravity. All of this can happen as long as the airplane flies quickly enough.

In a race, skippers follow different courses as they tack to try to find the strongest winds to propel them.

Scientists now know that a similar effect takes place on a sailboat. As the sail fills with the wind hitting it at an angle, the air traveling over the front of the sail has to travel farther than the air at the back of the sail. This creates low air pressure in front of the sail that "lifts" the boat forward. Lift can happen even if the wind is blowing in the opposite direction. The keel has a similar shape as an airplane wing and generates lift underwater. This helps drag the boat forward. For this reason, a sailor can make steady progress even in the face of strong winds.

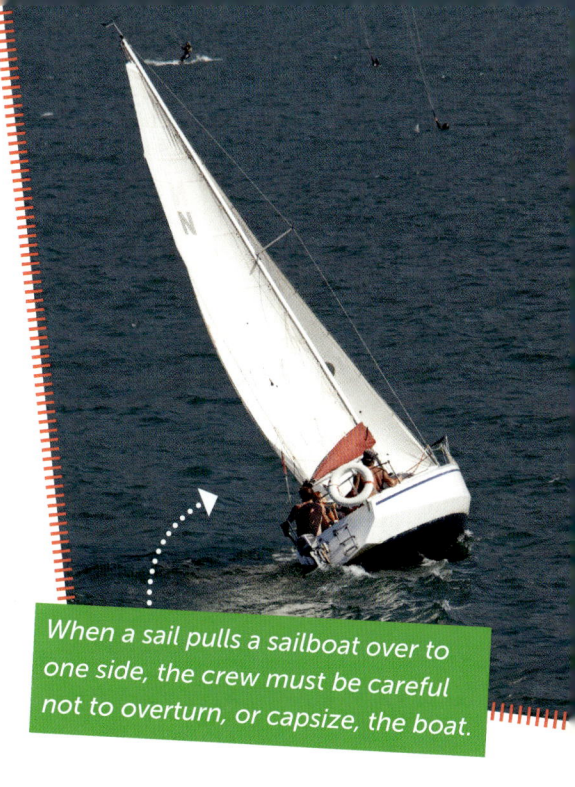

When a sail pulls a sailboat over to one side, the crew must be careful not to overturn, or capsize, the boat.

Indirect Course

Sailboats travel in a series of alternating zigzags, known as tacking. With tacking, the boat's nose continues to get turned into the wind. Most sailboats can sail, at most, within about 35 to 45 degrees to the wind. By tacking carefully, a sailor can maximize a boat's chance of catching the wind and moving forward.

During tacking, there is a moment when the sail is edge-on to the wind. The sail flaps loosely until it swings enough to fill with wind again. The boat's **inertia** carries it forward.

SCIENCE WINS!

ACROSS THE ATLANTIC

In 2016, a 100-foot (30 m) long yacht named Comanche crossed the Atlantic Ocean from the United States to Great Britain in a new record time. The trip took 5 days, 14 hours, 21 minutes, and 25 seconds. That was more than a day quicker than the previous record. Comanche is designed for speed. It is so wide at its stern that its crew called it the "aircraft carrier." The boat's mast is set more than halfway back along its length, with a huge boom that extends over the stern. The angle of the keel can be changed beneath the boat, which helps Comanche lean to one side or the other. When it lifts out of the water as it leans, the yacht has the same surface area in contact with the water as a craft only half its size. This smaller surface area reduces resistance and increases its speed.

CHAPTER 6

SURFING

On beaches where large waves roll toward the shore, surfers gather offshore. They wait in the water to catch a perfect wave when it starts to break. As a wave enters the shallows, it loses its shape and its top begins to tumble forward ahead of the rest. When that happens, the wave creates a tubelike space called a barrel. Surfers paddle with their hands to gain momentum, then jump up onto their feet to be carried to shore by the breaking wave.

> Surfers move their boards by using torque created by twisting their bodies around the waist.

Laws of Motion

Surfing relies on Newton's Laws of Motion, especially the First and Third Laws. According to the First Law, objects in motion tend to stay in motion. This same law says objects that are stationary tend to remain stationary. The Third Law, which says that every action has an equal and opposite reaction, is why surfers can control their boards so that they stay upright. If a surfer pushes down on one side of the board, that edge sinks and pushes into the water. The water pushes back with equal force and causes the board to turn.

Catching a Wave

The key to successful surfing is finding the right wave. Some beaches around the world are famous for them, such as the Banzai Pipeline off Oahu in Hawaii. These waves break over an offshore reef to form a barrel that surfers can ride inside.

Waves are energy in motion. The water itself moves up and down, as rolling energy moves through it. The energy comes from winds blowing out at sea. These winds create peaks and caps on the surface. If a wind blows hard enough, the peaks and caps form into rounded swells that begin to travel in the same direction. When they reach shallower water, near the shore, these swells become breaking waves. As the bottom gets shallower, the swells slow down and group closer together. The front of the wave becomes taller. The back of the wave keeps its shape. The ocean floor and the waves' own energy push the waves taller. Eventually, the front of the wave slows down so much that the back of the wave spills over it. Surf's up!

White surf is created as a wave's back edge catches up with the front edge. This is the ideal point for a surfer to "catch a wave."

Board and Balance

A surfer waits to catch the right wave off the coast of Tasmania, Australia, where breakers form tunnels that surfers can ride.

A board helps surfers to stay out of the water so they can move faster. This is because water has more drag on a moving object than the air does. Boards stay afloat from buoyancy, because they are less dense than the water. They also float because of the close molecules in the water. This forms a strong layer at the surface of the water known as surface tension.

All Aboard!

There are different kinds of surfboards. A longboard can be up to 12 feet (3.7 m) long. A shortboard is usually from 5 to 7 feet (1.5 to 2 m) long. Longboards are more stable, but shortboards are easier to use with waves. For a long time, surfboards were made of very light wood called balsa. Many modern boards are made from polystyrene or polyurethane foam. The boards float because they are less dense than the water beneath them. They are sealed with fiberglass and resin, which stops water from soaking into the board, which would make it heavy and eventually cause it to sink.

Boards sometimes have fins beneath them. Fins help with stability and steering. The bottom of the board can be flat. The board can also be rounded at the edges or at the front and back to reduce how much of the surface is in the water. The less of the board that touches the water, the less drag the water has on the board. This makes the board quicker for when it skims across the waves.

The board's fin pushes against the water, which pushes back, changing the direction in which the board is traveling.

Moving with Gravity

Once the surfer is riding a wave, they can steer by adjusting their center of gravity. They can adjust by moving their feet around on the board. Moving toward the back of the board lifts the front out of the water. Moving forward has the opposite effect. Leaning one way pushes the side of the board, known as the rail, into the water. The water pushes back and causes the board to turn the other way. Surfers often ride in a type of squat that keeps their center of mass lower. Lowering their center of mass keeps them from falling off the board.

SCIENCE WINS!

RECORD WAVE

In 2018, a British surfer named Tom Butler claimed to have surfed a 100-foot (30 m) wave at Nazaré in Portugal. Huge waves of that size only happen in a few places in the world, where the shape of the coast encourages large swells. For surfers, riding these waves is a challenge. They must be towed out through the surf by a motorboat or jet ski. Then they wait to catch the right wave. Once they are on their feet, they go down at high speed. Some surfers who fall or "wipe out" at such speeds suffer the effects of post-traumatic stress disorder (PTSD), a psychological condition usually suffered by people who have been in wars or huge disasters.

GET PHYSICAL!

It is time to find out for yourself something about the science of aquatic sports. In this experiment, you will learn about how water resistance affects how an object behaves in water.

YOU WILL NEED:
- Tall, clear plastic container, such as a plastic bottle
- Tape
- Ruler
- Raisins
- Table knife
- Watch or phone with a timer

Instructions

1. Take any labels off your empty bottle and wash it out.

2. Use tape to fasten the ruler to the outside of the bottle, so that one end touches the table. Position the ruler so the lower numbers are at the top and the higher numbers are at the bottom.

3. Fill the container with water. Try to make sure the surface of the water lines up with a whole number on the ruler. This makes it easier to measure.

4. Place one raisin on top of the water. Use your watch or phone to time how long it takes the raisin to reach the bottom of the bottle. Make a note of the time and the distance the raisin traveled.

5. Divide the distance the raisin traveled by the number of seconds it took to calculate its speed. (You can use a calculator if it helps.)

6. Repeat the experiment with another raisin, but this time cut the raisin into halves. Time how long it takes a half to reach the bottom of the bottle. Figure out its speed.

7. Try cutting a raisin into four quarters. Time how long a quarter takes to sink in the bottle. Calculate its speed.

8. Try cutting even smaller pieces of raisin and seeing how fast they travel through the water.

Analysis

Which size of raisin moves through the water faster? Why do you think this might be?

Conclusion

You probably found that the smaller pieces of raisin moved slower through the water. This is because of drag, or the friction caused by the water. The weight of the raisin causes it to sink because of gravity. The heavier the weight, the faster it sinks. At the same time, drag on the surface of the raisin slows it down. When you cut the raisin in two, each part has more than half the surface area of a whole raisin, but only half of its weight. This means the effect of drag is greater on the smaller pieces of raisin than the effect of gravity. As you cut the raisin into smaller pieces, the effect of drag increases compared to gravity.

This experiment shows that the less drag there is on a swimmer, the faster they can swim.

GLOSSARY

acceleration A change in velocity by speeding up, slowing down, or changing direction while in motion

air pressure The force exerted onto a surface by the weight of air

air resistance A force that acts in the opposite direction of an object traveling through the air and slows it down

atoms The smallest particles of matter

bearings Small metal balls that support turning parts of a machine

bow The front of a boat

buoyancy The ability of an object to float in water

center of mass The point in the middle of an object's mass

cylindrical Having a circular cross-section

deceleration A reduction in velocity

density How tightly packed something is

dinghies Small open boats with masts and sails

drag A force that opposes an object's motion

eddies Circular movements of water

energy The capacity for doing work

equilibrium point The depth at which a submerged object is balanced between gravity and buoyancy

force An interaction that changes the motion of something

friction The resistance of one object moving over another

fulcrum The point against which a lever is placed to turn

galleons Large, old-fashioned sailing ships

gravity A force that attracts things toward the center of Earth

impact The action of one object hitting another

inertia The quality of a moving body that makes it stay in motion or in a stationary body that makes it stay still

levers Bars resting on fulcrums, used to move loads

lift A pulling force created by lower pressure above an object

mass The quantity of matter in an object (its "weight")

molecules Particles made by atoms bonded together

momentum The quantity of motion of a body, equal to mass x velocity

perpendicular At a right angle to something

physics The branch of science that studies materials and energy

rotation point The central point around which an object turns

rudder A flat piece of wood or metal at the back of a boat, moved to control direction of travel

stern The back of a boat

streamlined Shaped to pass smoothly through air or water

submerged Under water

terminal velocity The maximum speed that an object can reach as it falls, when the upward drag force is equal to the downward gravity force

torque The force that causes objects to rotate

turbulence Unpredictable flow of fluids or air

velocity Speed in a specific direction

whitewater A turbulent area of water in a river

LEARNING MORE

Find out more about the physics of aquatic sports.

Books

Boudreau, Hélène. *Swimming Science* (Sports Science). Crabtree Publishing, 2009.

Hardman, Lizabeth. *Swimming* (Science Behind Sports). Lucent Books, 2011.

Lanser, Amanda. *The Science Behind Swimming, Diving, and Other Water Sports* (Science of the Summer Olympics). Capstone Press, 2016.

Yomtov, Neil. *The Science of a Cutback* (Full-Speed Sports). Cherry Lake Publishing, 2015.

Websites

Find out more about canoeing and the physics behind it at:
https://adventure.howstuffworks.com/outdoor-activities/water-sports/canoeing.htm

Read about the buoyancy force that makes objects float in water at:
www.khanacademy.org/science/physics/fluids/buoyant-force-and-archimedes-principle

Read about the forces acting on a sailboat and how sailors can use them at:
http://newt.phys.unsw.edu.au/~jw/sailing.html

Discover how divers make themselves spin faster in the air at:
www.wired.com/2012/08/diving-and-the-moment-of-inertia

INDEX

air pressure 32, 38
air resistance 17, 20
angular momentum 22, 43
Archimedes 7

backstroke 9, 10, 13
breaststroke 10, 13
buoyancy force 6, 7, 8, 9, 16, 17, 42
Butler, Tom 43
butterfly stroke 10, 12, 13

canoeing 24–27
catamarans 35
center of mass 9, 17, 29, 43
cliff diving 18, 21

displacement 7, 35
diving 18–23
drag 7, 10, 11, 13, 15, 17, 27, 29, 30, 34, 42, 43, 45

equilibrium point 7, 9

513XD dive 23
front crawl 10, 12, 13, 14–15
fulcrums 25, 28, 29, 37

galleons 36
gravity 6, 9, 16, 18, 19, 20–21, 38, 43, 45

hulls 33, 34–35
hydroplaning 30

impacts 18, 19, 21
inertia 22–23, 39

kayaking 24–27
keels 37, 38, 39

levers 4, 19, 25, 28, 29, 30, 37
lift 11, 14, 15, 16, 38
linear momentum 22
longboards 42

moment of inertia 22–23
momentum 22, 28, 29, 31, 39, 40, 43

Newton's Laws of Motion 9, 20, 26, 31, 37, 40

oars 24, 25, 28, 29, 30, 31

paddles and blades 24, 25, 26, 27

Phelps, Michael 13
post-traumatic stress disorder (PTSD) 43
pulleys 37

rotation point 22–23
rowing 24–31
rudders 33

sailing 32–39
sails 32, 33, 36–37, 38–39
shortboards 42
somersaults 18, 20, 22–23
springboards 19, 20
streamlining 11, 14, 15, 21, 26, 27
surfing 7, 40–43
swimming 4, 5, 6, 7, 8–17, 45
synchronized diving 21
synchronized swimming 17

tacking 38–39
terminal velocity 21
torque 22–23, 40
treading water 16
turbulence 27, 34

water polo 16–17
wave behavior 41
whitewater canoeing and kayaking 5, 25